TAKE YOUR BEST SHOT
A SPORTING CLAYS AND WINGSHOOTING PRIMER

BOOK ONE

DANIEL L. SCHINDLER

TAKE YOUR BEST SHOT
A SPORTING CLAYS AND WINGSHOOTING PRIMER

©Copyright 1994 by Daniel L. Schindler

Manufactured in the *United States of America*

ISBN: 1-885012-00-4

Printed by:
Jednota Press
A Division of Jednota Communications, Inc.
Rosedale Ave. & Jednota Lane
Middletown, PA 17057

Illustrations: Rosanne Wolf
Cover: Adrianne Camasta Kihm

FOREWORD

By
John Higgins
National Sporting Clays Association
Chief Instructor

With "TAKE YOUR BEST SHOT" Dan Schindler has bravely put his wingshooting thoughts into the written word. This book represents a mine of information for any shooting enthusiast.

To focus on the sheer fun of learning to shoot a shotgun, combined with how to be safe, is so important. Shooting, like any other sport, should be fun. The best way to learn and be safe, is to be relaxed and attentive in the company of a good coach. Shooting technique is simply all about building sight pictures. Combine this with positive feedback from the success of hitting targets, and learning to shoot becomes remarkably instinctive and great fun.

With this book, Dan Schindler, in a sincere and professional manner, successfully tackles the shooter's biggest fears - intimidation, pain, and above all, the fear of missing. He takes the shooter carefully, step by step through the learning stages, hopeful to avoid the many pitfalls along the way. Dan's precise, logical approach builds valuable confidence, and ensures that the sound foundation of correct basics is both remembered and enjoyed by shooters of all ages.

I hope this book will inspire you to ask many questions, as well as help lay a foundation for your lifelong interest in shotgun sports. However, be warned - the only cure is more of the same!

DEDICATION:
To Amy and Jenny; and my father, Toby.

ACKNOWLEDGMENTS
If it weren't for the N.S.C.A. programs; the patience and support of John Higgins, Jerry Meyer, Gil Ash, Dan Carlisle, Butch Roberson; all my supportive students; the sterling instructors I've certified; and Stefan, David, Ron, Henry, Barry, and Roy—this book would have been about chili recipes or battery maintenance.

CONTENTS

INTRODUCTION

Over the last few years, I've watched the sporting clays industry grow at a phenomenal rate. It reminds me of the '60s when debates raged over the best caliber, and outdoor writers filled volumes with noisy African sunsets, exotic campfire delicacies and five hundred yard kills. From boots to vehicles, promises were stretched to mesh with shooter's dreams. Manufacturers reaped the harvest from great marketing strategies. Writers and retailers had a field day with guns and quoted ballistics that pried wallets from tight pockets. It was exciting, and a great time was had by all.

Sporting clays is rekindling much of this same excitement. A fresh chapter in shooting history is upon us, rich in new products that again promise to fill your every wish. Limits are set only by one's pocket book and imagination. Quality traps, arms, accessories and reloading equipment fill every trading post to the brim.

*   *   *   *   *

Do I Need Instruction?

In many cases American products are superior. Yet, in spite of the fact that respectable wingshooting is unquestionably a learned skill, American shooters lag behind when it comes to attitudes toward instruction.

Superb competitors from other major countries recognize the value and necessity of competent teaching. Except in the US.

Why? Because we are plagued by two basic misconceptions.

First, many American males played the role of cowboy or soldier when they were young. Guns played a major role in our heritage. This heritage has been re-enacted megamillions of times by youngsters on every block. Wyatt Earp, the Lone Ranger, Billy the Kid and John Wayne were just a few of the legends that left indelible memories on each of us. They were supposedly fast on the draw and never missed their target. For many of us, this became an American tradition, and it became our Achilles heel.

Tutored by Grandpa in the duck blind and corn fields, many of these same youngsters read every article available on guns and hunting. Elmer Keith, Jack O'Connor, Grits Gresham, John Wooters and other popular writers wrote informative, stimulating articles that took us from the dark timber of the brown bear to the high meadows of the dall sheep. From the 1930s through the 1980s, the American outdoorsman began to believe the *mis*conception that being a good shot was his birthright.

Now Jack Goodshot finds himself standing on a sporting clays course for the first time. Eager and brimming with expectations, breaking less than 50% on his first try comes as a surprise. Ducks, geese, pheasants and quail have fallen in front of his gun. What happened on this course today?

Driving home, Jack convinces himself that all he needs is a little **p-r-a-c-t-i-c-e**. The second misconception has taken hold. Endless practice is substituted for quality instruction. Practice that reinforces his bad habits, day after day.

Wanting to shoot better, and going nowhere fast, Jack looks to professional instruction. This is the turning point. For the first time, he will learn the correct fundamentals. Measurable progress is just around the corner.

Congratulations. With this book, like Jack, you've taken the first real step toward better scores.

BEFORE WE BEGIN

SAFETY - FIRST PRIORITY

Sporting clays safety regulations are simple, and your adherence to these rules will be appreciated by those people sharing the range with you. Here are the most important safety regulations:

1. **NEVER** load your gun until you are in the shooter's box, and the muzzle is pointed down range.
2. Always make sure your gun is unloaded, action open, before you turn around to step out of the shooters box.
3. Load only one shell, for each target being presented, unless you are told otherwise.
4. Unless you are in the box shooting, your gun action must be open at all times.
5. Alcoholic beverages and shooting should always be kept separate.
6. Obey posted regulations for eye and ear protection.

It is most important that you understand all the basic rules covering gun safety, before you walk onto any firearms range. Your obeying these rules protects everyone. As you make plans to visit your local course, it should please you to know that these rules are being enforced at each of the many courses I've attended.

EYE DOMINANCE

If you shoot right handed, it is crucial that your right eye is your dominant eye; opposite for left. If you are not sure, please do the test explained on page 37.

SEEING THE GUN MUZZLE

Speaking in general terms, you can see objects with two types of vision. First is your primary vision. Using your **primary** vision, the object of your attention should be in focus. Various things around that object are slightly blurred, but can be seen with **peripheral** vision.

When you are shooting, which is visually clearest: the target or the barrel? If the answer is the barrel, please see comments on page 38.

SHOOTING WITH ONE EYE CLOSED

If you close one eye before you shoot, please see comments on page 38.

CHOOSE YOUR WEAPON CAREFULLY

Because men are usually larger and heavier than women and youths, they have the mass to absorb more recoil. Hence the 12 gauge is the preferred and most effective choice. The over and under shotgun is far and away the most popular, for a host of good reasons. The semiauto comes in a distant second, but not without its staunch supporters. Provided you keep them clean for reliability, their recoil reduction feature can be a definite advantage for many shooters. Though great for hunting purposes, the pump gun loses its edge when two clay birds appear.

For women and youths who are just entering sporting clays, it's probably a toss up over which is best, the 20 or 28 gauge. I slightly favor the 28 gauge myself, but feel the 20 gauge is also an excellent choice. Both are smaller framed guns that fit petite hands, and recoil is substantially reduced when the right loads are chosen. The semiauto will reduce recoil even further, especially for children or small framed individuals. Here again, I feel the break open shotgun carries the advantage on safety and dependability.

The experienced shooter often questions the use of a smaller gauge for the novice. In his opinion, we are handicapping the beginner. What this person is usually referring to is the reduced amount of shot being placed on the target. From a narrow perspective, he's right. But there are much more important considerations. First is our novice's questionable ability to handle a larger gun, and second is the increased recoil.

So a novice takes the liabilities of using a smaller gauge and actually turns them into assets. With the gun's lighter weight, smaller frame and diminished recoil, these gauges turn out to be **more** effective in the right hands. Skeptics can observe this phenomenon anytime. My experience with beginners has repeatedly proven the value and effectiveness of the lighter gauges. I've seen targets break, again and again.

As confidence increases and the recoil intimidation factor dissipates, your shooter will soon want to go to a 12 gauge. Just don't go there too soon! It may turn out to be an unpleasant experience, and our sport may have lost a great shooter.

LIST OF ILLUSTRATIONS

CHAPTER ONE

GUN CONTROL—YOURS

Our mutual goal is to help you become a better wingshot. Accordingly, each chapter is the foundation for the chapters that follow. The two lessons in chapter one are the shortest, most effective path to higher scores.

LESSON 1: Doing Your Homework

Most beginners call for a target, and then develop a strategy to break it. But clay targets don't give us the luxury of time. Beginners miss because they are thinking **during** the shot. Too much thinking, after the target is launched, is counter-productive. A strategy must be in place **before** calling for that clay bird. Doing Your Homework is the thinking part of the shot. It's your set up. Always, do your planning and finish your set up, before you say pull.

When that target appears, it's time to shoot, not think.

Have you ever noticed that the harder one tries to break a target, the more difficult it becomes? Just the thought of missing can tighten muscles. In simple terms, the more preoccupied we become about breaking the target, the more we get side-tracked from our real mission on the firing line, and one target after another floats into the grass, untouched.

"Hey Dan, I just want to break the target. I don't have time to

NO
- Don't Miss
- First Place Trophy
- Must Win Today

YES
- Good Set Up—No Mistakes
- Focus on the Target

DIAGRAM 1—STRATEGY

get my Ph.D. in Shooting Physics."

I hear you.

But let's look at the shot carefully. It happens quickly, doesn't it? Pull, bang, and watch the target break. We hope. Now, let's run that back in slow motion. Breaking the target consistently requires combining: (1) a pre-planned, precise set-up; (2) a one piece coordinated gun mount; (3) sufficient muzzle speed; (4) the right sight picture; (5) the correct lead; and (6) exact timing on the trigger pull. Is it any wonder we make mistakes during a shot that takes less than 1.5 seconds on 2 targets?

LESSON 2: Gun Control

What is it, exactly, that breaks a target?

The shot string.

And how does the shot string get to the target?

You have to put it there.

A beautiful stock, custom loads, a new vest, wanting first prize, determination, peer admiration, none of these things will break a target. Somehow, some way, consistently, **YOU** have to put that shotstring on that target.

Let's take an objective look at the concept of control. Considering that the gun and shot string are not attached to the target, it is impossible for you to influence or control the target in any way whatsoever. The only **link** between the shooter and the target, is the gun and ammunition. You **can** exert control over your gun and ammunition, but not the target. So the shooter's job is not to break the target, but to deliver the shot string *to* the target.

Everything you do before you pull the trigger has a direct affect on the outcome of the shot. Thinking about first place, wanting to win, money, how many have I missed so far, only lead you further and further away from accurately directing that shot string to the target.

Separating the "task" from the "result" is the starting point for successful shooting. Breaking targets consistently requires concentration on two things: SET UP and SHOT EXECUTION. Both of which we **can** control.

In sporting clays, your real objective should be to TAKE YOUR BEST SHOT.

SUMMARY:

1.) Do all your planning and finish your set up before the target is launched.
2.) To Take Your Best Shot, you must be focused on set up, and shot execution.

CHAPTER TWO

MISS MANAGEMENT

Now we know our objective. Set up and shot execution is the path to a broken target. But suppose the target doesn't break?

We need to define a missed target. The rule book states a "visible piece" is scored a "dead" target. When a visible piece is not seen, the target is scored as "lost." Marked as a "0" on the score sheet. And right there is where the trouble often begins.

A miss is the little gremlin in the sporting clays world. Every time you miss a target, this gremlin has the power to make you angry. Anger is a negative emotion, and negative emotions fracture your concentration. Performance crumbles. This is a serious mistake, folks.

What does all of this look like on your score sheet? The target you just missed will now cause your next miss. And so on, until you regain control.

But, you do have a choice. You can continue to allow a missed target to intimidate and influence your next shot, or you can dismiss it and focus on breaking the next pair. Since tournaments are won by breaking targets, and we're both working hard to get you to better scores, the correct choice is obvious.

I too once struggled with this. Now, when I miss an important target, the word *choice* comes to mind immediately. Many of my students smile when they miss. They won't allow the miss to take control. They take that miss and channel their feelings into being **more focused** on the next shot.

Misses can be troublesome. A miss will probably be coming your way shortly. If not, please call your new agent, this retiring author.

An integral part of our sport, everybody gets their share of misses. So what should we do with them? The best way to approach them is from the positive, not the negative.

I suggest, in the very beginning, you don't count them. This is practice. Concentrate on the mechanics of the shot. Focus on the targets you **do** break. Your mission is to improve form and strive for good repetition. By not counting misses, you relieve the pressure they cause. That's effective, confidence building, "miss" management.

Here's the question. Can you call for this next target, and not think about missing it? Can you concentrate only on good form? When you answer this question "yes", you've taken a giant step forward. It's a scientific fact: positive thinking breaks more targets.

Missing can be turned to your advantage. When misses occur, ask yourself why? A student with a solid understanding of shooting fundamentals can give the answer. Knowing why you missed will allow you to make the correction, and kill the remaining targets.

As a teaching tool, misses provide opportunities to learn.

Misses will always be around, so we might as well make the best of them. Learn as much from them as you can, and keep them in their proper perspective. "Miss" management is a crucial part of your game.

SUMMARY:

1.) Don't count your misses. Focus on the targets you break!
2.) When you miss, figure out why, and make the correction.
3.) Don't allow a miss to control your next shot.

CHAPTER THREE

THE RIGHT TOOL FOR THE JOB

In our hurry to shoot, many of us stop thinking about our equipment when we reach the first Field. The impulse to step into the box before we're ready can set up a miss, even before the target is launched. Calling for a target and being unprepared will explain a long row of zeros on the score sheet.

Choosing the best chokes and ammunition doesn't have to be complicated. This book gives you what I call down-in-the-dirt, results oriented advice. Procedures that are simple, and **effective**. The following recommendations are dependable, easy to use, and grind clay targets into itty-bitty pieces.

Here is one way to be prepared.

Outside the shooter's box, you should be analyzing the target flight path, angle, distance and speed. Each target can best be broken in a specific spot or place; possibly in the trees, against the sky, or on the ground. Locate that spot.

That location, translated into a distance, dictates the proper choke selection and shot size.

For the majority of sporting clays targets in our country (which range from ten to thirty yards off the muzzle), **cylinder bore** and **skeet choke** should be our workhorse chokes. This includes rabbit targets. For singles, or the second bird in a pair that crosses the twenty-five yard mark, improved cylinder is perfect. For medium range targets between thirty and forty yards, slightly more choke may be appropriate. This is discussed in TAKE YOUR BEST SHOT, Book II.

Shot sizes vary, as do their performances. Check your reloading manual and look at the number of 9's in a 1 1/8 oz. load, versus the same load with 7 1/2's. There are approximately 275 more 9's. In the exact same load! But are 9's effective? Yes. Not only do 9's disintegrate targets with machine-like repetition, including rabbits, but the increased number of shot is a decided advantage on closer targets. Inside 25 yards, 9's (or 8 1/2's) won't let you down.

8's and 7 1/2's find their niche on targets over twenty-five yards. Both are dependable when placed correctly. Demonstrations have shown that 2 3/4 dram loads of 7 1/2's will repeatedly break targets beyond 45 yards.

There are advantages and disadvantages to the various shot loads, ranging from 7/8 oz. of shot to 1 1/8 oz. On closer targets, I somewhat favor the 1 oz. because it seems to capture the best features of all other sporting clays loads. Especially reduced recoil. Generally superior patterns, increased velocities at moderate pressures, and superb target breaking ability at all reasonable ranges are other pluses. When the yardage does extend beyond forty, an acceptable argument can be made for heavier loads of powder and shot.

There is merit in walking onto a course with two different loads to handle the variety of targets you may face.

Some sporting clays ranges provide all the challenge you can handle. Using tighter chokes and larger shot, on close, fast targets, is a decided handicap. Why make the sport harder? The same goes for heavy dram loads when not necessary. They too have their place, but not on closer targets.

In factory ammunition, the Winchester Lites and Super Lites are excellent. At my home course — The Warrington Club in Wellsville, PA — the Winchester Lites will break a particularly long tower shot with ease. Their reduced recoil is a definite advantage, and both factory loads literally hammer targets.

At the reloading bench, the manuals are worth their weight in gold. Many sincere thanks to the competent people who provide this essential information. I follow the charts to the letter. For me, however, the true test of any load is in the field. It's worth the time and effort to pattern your load for density, dispersion and point of impact. Testing your load for felt recoil is also recommended.

Let a manual and common sense guide you to the load that best suits your personal needs. The right choke and shot in your gun put the odds in your favor. After all, strategy is half the game.

SUMMARY:

1.) The majority of targets in the US are under 30 yards. Make your cylinder bore and skeet chokes your workhorse chokes.

2.) 9's and 8 1/2's are deadly on closer targets when coupled with open chokes.

3.) Consider the lighter recoiling loads like the Winchester Lites.

4.) Use tighter chokes and 8's and 7 1/2's for medium to long targets.

1st
Break
Point

2nd
Break
Point

DIAGRAM 2—BREAK POINTS

CHAPTER FOUR

NUMBER 1:
THE BREAK POINT

Targets not only come in assorted sizes, but fly in unorthodox patterns, irregular speeds and confusing distances. Add a little drop, curve or angle into the equation, and it's no wonder shooters talk to themselves. But every fair target can be broken. Sporting clays targets penalize an errant swing, and reward a resourceful strategy.

To develop an effective game plan for breaking these birds, there has to be a common denominator; a place to begin. Thankfully, there is. Whether the target is on the ground or in the air, every single target has a point, or spot on its path of travel, **where it is most vulnerable to being broken**. This spot will be referred to as **NUMBER 1**, and is called the **BREAK POINT**.

A break point must be established for each target, including the second target on a pair. This spot, or spots on doubles, helped you pick your chokes and shot size before you stepped into the box.

Once in the box, very specific preparations can begin to set you up *physically* for the shot. Looking out across your field of fire, trace the target's flight path with your eyes, and zero in on each break point. Don't concern yourself with the size of the area, or try to measure it. Where your eye is focusing, that is the break point. See diagram 2.

The most important shot is the **first one**. Break that target as close to its break point as possible. This will allow you the maximum time available for the second target.

Here are a few tips on Break Points:

1.) Choose your own break points. Your choice may be different, possibly better, than someone else's.

2.) Occasionally, reversing the order in which everyone else attempts a pair, may have an advantage. So watch carefully.

3.) Don't pick a break point too close, or too far, from the trap. Too close, and the target is still a blur in your vision. Get it in focus first, then take your shot when you're ready. Pick a break point too far from the trap, and your swing is slowing down. You will probably shoot behind the target. The sweet spot is in the middle of these two extremes.

4.) Try not to fight a target's speed. Pick a break point **just a little** further down the target path where you have a better shot. This is often true on rabbits. Usually, a target broken slightly down the path has less risk, and will give you a better chance to get your X.

5.) On a fast target where you have no choice, pick the earliest break point with which you are comfortable. Every millisecond beyond that point increases the yardage from your muzzle, changing the shot from medium to long.

6.) Be careful on incoming overhead. Don't pick a late break point. The target may get past you. The late break point is also at the top (and the end) of your swing, greatly increasing the probability of a shot behind the target.

Remember, to TAKE YOUR BEST SHOT, we're building a shooting system, A sequence that builds easy, skillful repetition. A sequence that is specifically designed to remove all excess, wasteful movement in your attack on the target. Minimizing movement minimizes mistakes. Getting down to zero mistakes = Xs.

So it is critical that you pick your break points in order to set up the shot. Without them, your shot can be careless and haphazard. With a little experience, choosing them wisely is not difficult.

SUMMARY:
   1.) Establishing the break point(s) is necessary to begin your set up.
   2.) Break points assist with choke and shot size selection.

Doing Your Homework

Number 1   Break Point

CHAPTER FIVE

NUMBER 2: FOOT POSITION

> ❖ Beginning now, all directions for feet and hands are given for a right handed person. Lefty's, please reverse.

Have you ever tried to build the top of something before the bottom? In shooting, it works about as well. Therefore, place your feet properly in your set up. This enhances your swing. It prepares you to hit the target.

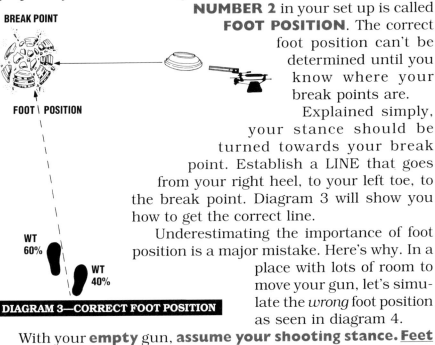

NUMBER 2 in your set up is called **FOOT POSITION**. The correct foot position can't be determined until you know where your break points are.

Explained simply, your stance should be turned towards your break point. Establish a LINE that goes from your right heel, to your left toe, to the break point. Diagram 3 will show you how to get the correct line.

Underestimating the importance of foot position is a major mistake. Here's why. In a place with lots of room to move your gun, let's simulate the *wrong* foot position as seen in diagram 4.

DIAGRAM 3—CORRECT FOOT POSITION

With your **empty** gun, **assume your shooting stance. Feet ARE POINTED SLIGHTLY TOWARDS THE IMAGINARY TRAPPER.** In slow motion, as you swing to the left, can you feel your hips lock?

Repeating the swing at normal speed, can you feel your swing slow down?

Because your hips lock up and your muzzle slows down, you

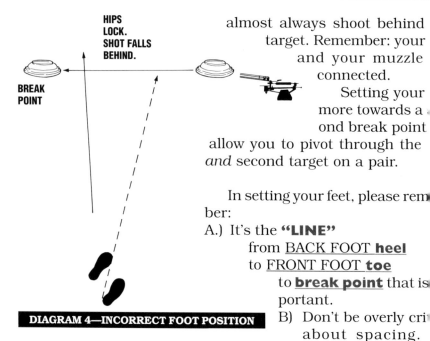

HIPS LOCK. SHOT FALLS BEHIND.

BREAK POINT

DIAGRAM 4—INCORRECT FOOT POSITION

almost always shoot behind target. Remember: your and your muzzle connected.

Setting your more towards a ond break point allow you to pivot through the *and* second target on a pair.

In setting your feet, please rem ber:

A.) It's the **"LINE"** from BACK FOOT **heel** to FRONT FOOT **toe** to **break point** that is portant.

B) Don't be overly cri about spacing.

shoulder width or slightly less. GET COMFORTA
C.) Don't measure. GET COMFORTABLE.
D.) For TWO break points, set foot position **LINE**, slig **more** towards **second** break point.
E.) Front knee slightly bent. Weight distribution: app mately 60/40,with 60% on the front foot.

Here's the shot in slow motion again.

When the targets appear and those feet are wrong: your lock up; your shoulders can't turn; the gun slows down; and shoot behind. Why didn't you notice this before? Because a this takes place in one to two seconds, and you were concen ing on breaking the targets.

Setting your feet correctly only takes a few seconds. B gets overlooked. A lot. Next time you miss, don't look at gun, look down at your feet.

SUMMARY:

1.) Stance should be towards the break point(s), not the trap-per. (Excluding incoming, of course.)
2.) Get comfortable.
3.) Get the **LINE** from heel➥ to toe➥ to breakpoint.

DOING YOUR HOMEWORK

NUMBER 1   BREAK POINT(S)

NUMBER 2   FOOT POSITION

CHAPTER SIX

NUMBER 3: MUZZLE HOLD

Have you noticed that the more experienced shooter breaks targets sooner, or earlier, than you do. The novice usually takes the shot further down the flight path, at longer yardages. This is due to excess gun movement in the early part of the swing. Much of the little time you did have was used to hunt for the target, which is escaping.
Hence the tardy shot, and longer yardages. How can you get on that target faster and earlier?

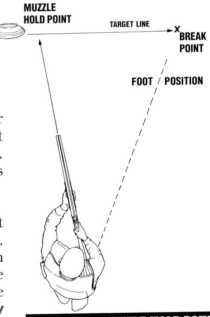

DIAGRAM 5—MUZZLE HOLD POINT

Having already chosen your break points (#1), your feet should now be properly set (#2), giving the hips and shoulders room to swing.

What's next?

Point the muzzle at the first break point. With the muzzle, trace the target's flight path in reverse, or backwards. The muzzle is moving towards the trap. As a general rule, **halfway** back to the trap would be a good starting place. Holding the muzzle very still, the critical question becomes this: Will the crossing target appear to fly directly over the muzzle, almost touching it? If so, you've achieved **NUMBER 3**, the correct **MUZZLE HOLD POINT**. See diagram 5.

One of the nicest surprises during a lesson comes after a broken target, when my student turns around with a broad smile and states, "That shot didn't seem hard." Because everything is

new, the student knows only how the shot feels, but not w
So, why does the shot feel so much easier?

Because the set up on the target is excellent. Having eve
thing in place assures the proper sequence, swing and tim
Numbers 1 (break points), 2 (foot position), and 3 (muzzle ho
are all correct. Naturally, when the swing begins, there is
any wasted motion. When the target appears and stock me
the cheek, the sight picture is perfect. At this point, no think
is required and it's time to pull the trigger.

Time used after the word pull: minimal.
Time wasted during the swing: none.
Mechanical errors: zero.
Results: XX.

"You mean the shot was faster?" In a sense, yes; but m
importantly, the shot was more efficient. There were no exc
movements or mistakes. It was pre-planned and under cont
The swing was smoother. So, yes, to an important degree,
shot was faster.

I'll grant you some flexibility on your break points and y
foot position. But not on your muzzle hold point. Every frac
of an inch your muzzle hold point is off the line (the visuali
target flight path) will cost you precious time in finding the
get. When the muzzle hunts for the target, time is wasted. T
that the target is using to escape.

Being off the line creates excess movement. That moven
creates mistakes. Mistakes = lost targets.

Because the targets are moving, muzzle speed is **ESSENT**
to breaking targets. Whether it's a tennis racket, a baseball
or a golf club, each must coil back to a certain point, or th
can be no swing. A crucial part of the shot is a swing that st
on the target flight path.

Now that we know to put the muzzle "on-the-line", lets
about how far back we take the muzzle. As stated earlier, a g
rule of thumb for a muzzle hold point is halfway back to
trap. I'm sure you will have to adjust this slightly as you
counter the wide variety of sporting clays presentations.

Getting the correct muzzle hold point requires concentra
during the set up. Whether the shot feels easy or hard is dire
proportionate to how accurately you placed your muzzle on-
line. Getting it right makes a huge difference when you att
that target.

❖ Take a moment and note how each step you've taken in the set up is dependent on the other. Notice how each one contributes to excellent shot mechanics. (A loose, careless set up results in poor mechanics. And we know where that leads.) Do Numbers 1 (break points), 2 (foot position), and 3 (muzzle hold) properly, and you've got a move on the target that is efficient, swift and deadly.

SUMMARY:
1.) The muzzle hold point is the most important part of the physical set up before the target is launched. Be precise.
2.) The target **LINE** (flight path) that helped you pick the muzzle hold point for most targets, should now guide the path of your swing.

DOING YOUR HOMEWORK

NUMBER 1   BREAK POINT(S)

NUMBER 2   FOOT POSITION

NUMBER 3   MUZZLE HOLD POINT

CHAPTER SEVEN

NUMBER 4:
FOCAL POINT

You're in the box on Field One. On your command, you can hear the trap release. Your hips and arms begin to move. The gun is rising. Oh yes, just one more thing. Consider doing all of this with your eyes **CLOSED**.

In sporting clays, the importance of vision is greatly underestimated. Your vision plays a vital role in breaking targets. The sooner you can see a target, the easier the shot becomes. Having the target in view as early as possible helps tremendously. With your eyes, hunt the target down **quickly**. Be aggressive with your eyes.

Establishing the break points (#1), we set our feet (#2), and muzzle hold point (#3). To finish the set up, move the eyes back to a spot WHERE THE TARGET WILL FIRST COME INTO FOCUS. This last step, **NUMBER 4**, is the **FOCAL POINT**. See diagram 6.

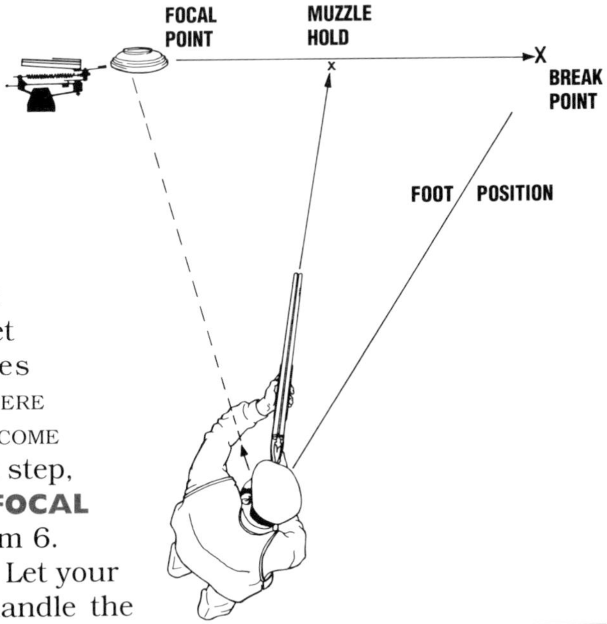

Be careful here. Let your peripheral vision handle the initial launch of the target which appears as a blur. If your eyes have to chase the target, chances are good the swing will go out of control.

Too many beginners move at the command "pull", or the sound

DIAGRAM 6—FOCAL POINT

of the trap. This is a mistake. The target hasn't come into vie
Where is the muzzle going?

There's nothing wrong with feeling intensity go up a note
when the bird is launched. But the real ON switch for moveme
is the visual focus on the target. Depending on the presentatio
the swing might start at that instant. Even if it doesn't, with tl
target in focus, the brain can begin to calculate speed, ang
and distance. Precious time is being used efficiently. The shot
going according to plan.

The majority of sporting clays shooters use only 50% of the
visual strengths. For example. Consider your misses on that la
quick report pair. Close your eyes and do an instant repla
Honestly, were you visually locked on each target, or did y
shoot at an orange **blur** both times?

Too often, novices lose focus on a fast target. When this ha
pens, they usually miss. Why? Because the beginner shoots a-
o-u-n-d the target. Shot placement must be good or you'll he
"lost a pair".

Seeing the target clearly starts your gun moving in tl
right direction.

Having done Numbers 1, 2, 3 and 4 properly (break poi
foot position, muzzle hold, focal point), your set up is comple
You are now programmed to break this target.

SUMMARY:
1. Be aggressive with your eyes. See the target as soon as possible.
2. Make sure the target is in focus when you shoot.

DOING YOUR HOMEWORK

NUMBER 1   BREAK POINT(S)

NUMBER 2   FOOT POSITION

NUMBER 3   MUZZLE HOLD POINT

NUMBER 4   FOCAL POINT

CHAPTER EIGHT

THE ATTACK

We've reached at a critical stage in the shot. Homework done, *the set up is complete.*

AT THIS POINT, IT IS ESSENTIAL THAT YOU MENTALLY DISMISS THE SET UP.

Any thoughts about set up, during the shot, divides your concentration and contributes to a miss. **100%** of your attention must be focused on the target, the insert and the correct sight picture.

DIAGRAM 7—GUN UP POSITION

PART 1: GUN UP

To simplify the shot, I highly recommend you begin with the gun premounted, or gun up. See diagram 7. Only in a tournament is gun down, or low gun required. **Don't** feel self conscious about your gun up position. This is just a starting point. For now, gun up is easier, and will help you break more targets. By your tenth box of shells, you'll probably be ready to try gun down.

If you have been shooting sporting clays for a while, and prefer gun down, proceed. The novice can only concentrate on so many things. After launch, targets give you little time to do anything. When the target appears, the less there is to think about the better. Gun up accomplishes this, by

DIAGRAM 8—GUN DOWN POSITION

eliminating a complicated step in the shot process. For first time people, gun up is preferred because it's faster, and fewer mistakes are made. From gun down, doing the mount incorrectly contributes to missing.

Gun down position, diagram 8, is covered in TAKE YOUR BEST SHOT, Book II.

Having done your homework, your set up on the target is complete. **Before** you say pull, consider what the visual relationship should be between the muzzle and the next speeding target.

Remember, focus on the bird, and let your peripheral vision handle the muzzle. This relationship between the target and the muzzle is called the **sight picture**. This picture can be different for everyone, depending on the shooting method.

PART 2: SHOOTING METHODS

Thinking about the shot, <u>after the target is in the air,</u> invites disaster. All that should remain is for you to focus on the clay and break it.

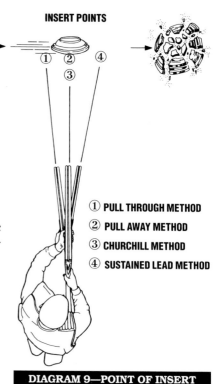

INSERT POINTS

① PULL THROUGH METHOD
② PULL AWAY METHOD
③ CHURCHILL METHOD
④ SUSTAINED LEAD METHOD

The target in sporting clays is always moving. So is your body and your gun. Somehow, we've got to get all of this lined up properly in order for you to score Xs. Homework finished, your body and gun are in the right place. Gun up has brought us to the completion of the shot.

Cheek raised slightly off the stock, eyes are looking back for the target. (Focal point.)

Time to say "pull."

The target appears.

The muzzle begins to move. Your DESTINATION with that muzzle is called the point of insertion, or **INSERT POINT**. For some, the insert point **(visual reference)** is

**DIAGRAM 9—POINT OF INSERT
FOR VARIOUS METHODS**

on the target. For others, it is in front or in back of the target. Knowing that insert point in advance, and achieving it during the attack, sets up the right sight picture. See diagram 9.

Because the target is moving, the shot string should be launched **ahead** of the target. The shot string is then on a path where it will intercept the target. It is this business of being in front of the target that we call **lead**.

For me, the word *lead* tends to imply *measurement.* Trying to measure a lead can slow your swing, resulting in a shot behind the target. To help a student see a lead, without measuring, I refer to the space between the target and the muzzle as the **window**. I refer to windows in terms of small, medium, a little larger, etc. For certain shooting methods, I ask my student to **"keep the window open"** at the point of pulling the trigger. See diagram 10. When this sight picture is achieved, chances are excellent the target will break.

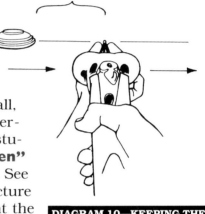

DIAGRAM 10—KEEPING THE WINDOW "OPEN"

Getting the correct lead on a target can be accomplished numerous ways. One person will see one sight picture over the muzzle, and another person will see something else. This takes us into one's personal shooting style, or method.

Generally speaking, there are four basic methods. Each method has its strengths and weaknesses.

With good reasons, **Sustained Lead** is a favorite method, promoted by many instructors. Basically, when the target appears, the muzzle is inserted in front of the target, and **stays in front of the target through the shot**. Lead is apparent as the stock reaches the cheek. Depending on your insert, you may have to adjust this visual lead. On the plus side for this method, lead is apparent quickly, because you build it in, during the insert. Putting a Sustained Lead on a target is relatively easy, providing a major benefit for many target presentations. The visual picture of the target-muzzle relationship is excellent.

Sustained Lead shooters often stop their gun when the trigger is pulled. To compensate for this, I remind them to visually "keep the window open" through the shot (don't allow the target to pass the muzzle). Doing so makes this method uncomplicated, and very effective.

The **Swing Through** method is also popular. Many shooters employ this method for both clay targets and live birds. The muzzle is inserted slightly behind the target. The muzzle is then swept through the target and the shot fired. Like a brush stroke, this is often referred to as painting the target. Sweeping the target builds muzzle speed, which is critical to breaking the target. This sweeping motion significantly helps the shooter who has a tendency to stop the gun. Because the muzzle is accelerating through the target, possibly lead may not be seen. Lead is provided however, by the increased muzzle speed. If the timing can be mastered, Swing Through can also be very effective.

The **Pull Away** method is similar to Swing Through. The two primary differences are (1) the insert is on the target, and (2) as you pull away from the target, lead can briefly be seen (not measured). The insert may be somewhat easier for you, and the Pull Away method also promotes good muzzle speed. Pull Away shooters should see a window opening up before firing.

The first three methods can be difficult to implement on a target that is A) very fast, or B) sneaking through obstacles. This brings us to the fourth method, which lends itself very well to this hide-and-seek target.

My slightly modified **Churchill** method appears to dispense with visual lead. Explained as simply as possible, the shot is attempted directly at the target. Churchill may appear fast, but, done correctly, should feel smooth and under control. Ample arm movement and muzzle speed are two priorities. The effectiveness of Churchill has been established for many years and is well worth learning.

Which method is best? The one that is easiest for you. The method that feels comfortable to the student is usually the most effective. Because people are different, I teach all four methods. Sustained Lead and Pull Away seem to be utilized the most. Any one of these methods will break targets reliably.

As you progress, you'll notice that certain targets are best approached with a particular method. If not already in use, I like to introduce Churchill in follow up lessons. Eventually, learning a second or third method will give you choices to handle any clay target you may encounter.

Regardless of the method chosen, the learning process involves missing targets. Certain problems are more common than others, but each can be remedied with a little concentration and effort.

My experience has shown that most misses occur due to insufficient lead on the target. Stopping the gun is the biggest offender. Keeping the window open, or accelerating the muzzle past the target is the easiest and most effective correction.

Frequently, a student consistently fires at a target late. At that point in the swing, the muzzle is decellerating, and the shot arrives behind the target. If you find yourself doing this, try to remember this simple strategy. Take your entire swing (not the bird flight), from start to finish, and break it down into thirds; first third, middle third and last third. If you are pulling the trigger in the last third of the swing, your chances of hitting the target are drastically reduced. Take the shot during the middle third of your swing. Invariably, you will find your break point(s) in the middle third of your swing plane, not the last third.

Though we shoot for fun and the enjoyment of watching targets break, practice requires a reasonable degree of concentration and discipline. Getting the right sight picture is paramount. And though you can see the target and muzzle through the shot, it's possible you may not be aware of the mechanical errors you're making. Here is where an instructor's guidance becomes invaluable. The instructor's eyes will see what you can't, saving valuable time, energy and ammunition.

With homework done, and the set up complete, here is a summary on the attack:

1.) If possible, start in the gun up position.
2.) Release all thoughts about set up.
3.) TELL YOURSELF what method you are going to apply on this target - THEN say pull.
4.) The muzzle must be pushed to the correct **INSERT POINT**. See Diagram 9.
5.) With the **target** in focus, get the right sight picture and pull the trigger. See Diagram 10.

IN ORDER FOR THE TARGET TO BREAK, THE SIGHT PICTURE MUST BE RIGHT BEFORE YOU PULL THE TRIGGER.

CHAPTER NINE

MAKING IT ALL WORK

As we look back over the previous chapters, the information may appear a bit overwhelming. It isn't. Doing Your Homework eliminates the excess and wasted movements most shooters use in their approach. It is your precise set up that makes the shot **EASIER**, not harder. This allows you to find the bird quickly, swing without mistakes, and break the target consistently.

As this book comes to a close, a short review might help. Let's take a look at the fundamentals.

THE 10 MOST IMPORTANT FUNDAMENTALS

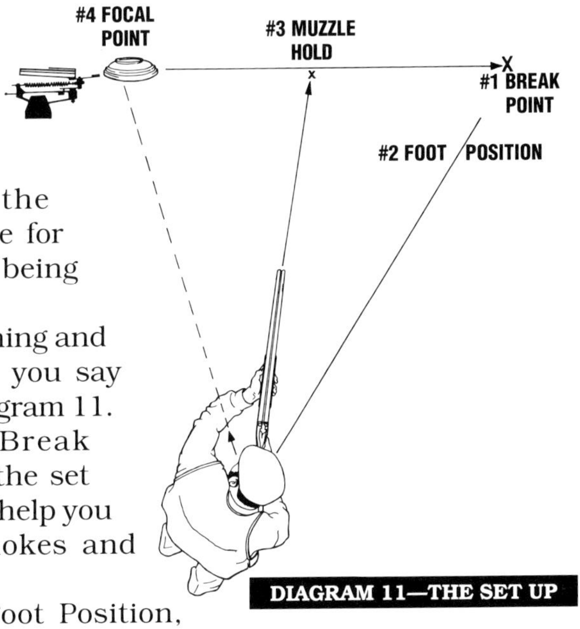

I. Choose the right choke and use a load with low to moderate recoil. Pick the right shot size for the distance being attempted.

#4 FOCAL POINT

#3 MUZZLE HOLD

#1 BREAK POINT

#2 FOOT POSITION

II. Do your planning and set up before you say "pull." See diagram 11.

III. Number 1, Break Points, start the set up. They also help you pick your chokes and loads.

DIAGRAM 11—THE SET UP

IV. Number 2, Foot Position, will help keep that gun moving.

V. Number 3, Muzzle Hold, gets you on the target fast!

VI. Number 4, Focal Point, is the ON switch. Be aggressive with your eyes. If you're late here, the rest of the shot will be late too.

VII. Homework finished, **before** you say pull, rehearse the insert point.

❖**The set up is complete! MENTALLY SHIFT GEARS. Say pull and look for that target!**

VIII. With the target in focus (see diagram 12), go to your insert point.

IX. Using your method, get the right sight picture.

X. **Pull the trigger!**

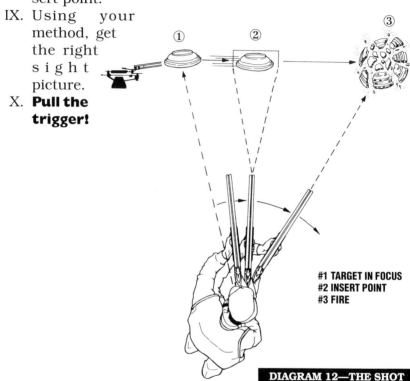

#1 TARGET IN FOCUS
#2 INSERT POINT
#3 FIRE

DIAGRAM 12—THE SHOT

THE SHOT CONDENSED:

SET UP (DIAGRAM 11)
Find your break point(s).
Set your feet.
Set your muzzle.
Look back.

ATTACK (DIAGRAM 12)
Go to your insert point.
Get the right sight picture.
FIRE!

As we conclude, you should know that your efforts to improve are admirable. You are to be heartily commended. The learning process will provide you with rewards beyond a broken target.

TAKE YOUR BEST SHOT has furnished you with the components of the shot. The individual, essential parts. Just like balancing, steering and pedaling a bicycle must all be coordinated, so must the steps in executing a successful shot.

Having read these chapters and learned what to do in the box, the process of integrating these steps can be significantly accelerated when complemented by professional instruction. Whereas practicing good fundamentals on your own can achieve positive results, a patient, competent instructor can render hands-on guidance, direction and the benefit of many years of experience.

Knowledge of the fundamentals is indispensable. Bridging the gap from knowledge to skill is best achieved with a certified instructor.

CONGRATULATIONS.
You're on your way to Taking Your Best Shot.
So, I'll meet you on Field One with a trapper. Ready?

APPENDIX

COMMON PROBLEMS

EYE DOMINANCE

On moving targets, a shotgun is pointed, not aimed. Therefore, it is extremely important to get the gun aligned with the dominant eye, or the eye over the barrel. This allows the gun and the eye to be focused on the exact same point. That's why it's impossible for a right handed shooter to hit a target consistently, if he is left eye dominant, and vice versa.

To determine which of your eyes is dominant, here is a simple test. See diagram 13.

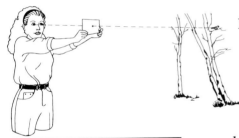

DIAGRAM 13—DOMINANT EYE

Take a card or piece of paper about 4"x 5", and push a pencil hole through the middle of it. Look for a small object like a bird on a limb, a knob on your TV or stereo, the top of a fence post, or something similar. With both hands, hold the card at arm's length. Find the object and place it in the hole, **keeping both eyes open**. DON'T lose sight of the object. Bring the card back to your face. The card should automatically go to your dominant eye. Repeat the test to make sure.

If the test reveals that your dominant eye is opposite the shoulder you use to shoot, all is not lost. Many folks shoot very well with this condition. The following can help:

    A. If we have a new and inexperienced shooter, consider changing hands and shooting from the other shoulder. Though awkward at first, switching to the other shoulder can be the quickest and most effective solution.

B. If you have someone who's been shooting for awhile and finds changing hands almost impossible, consider placing a small patch over the shooting glasses' lens of the dominant eye. Not the entire glass. Just a small patch that effectively blocks the dominant eye during shooting. It only takes a few minutes. Don't be afraid to ask an instructor to help place the "dot" or patch.

C. Some people with this problem call for the bird with both eyes open. When the stock reaches the cheek, the dominant eye is then closed. This allows the other eye (over the barrel) to do the work and complete the shot.

SEEING THE GUN MUZZLE

Lots of folks see their barrel clearly, with the target out of focus. Because of this, the target is always outracing their muzzle. With insufficient muzzle speed, the shot arrives late, behind the target.

With a rifle and a pistol, we do look at the open sights. In the clay target sports, we don't. It's the opposite. The target must be in focus, not the barrel. Concentrate on the target. See it clearly, and keep it in focus.

SHOOTING WITH ONE EYE CLOSED

Though some people do it for good reasons, you are handicapping yourself when you shoot with one eye closed. Pointing a shotgun effectively is best done by instinct. Your brain computes target distances, speeds, angles, elevations, etc. from visual input. Closing one eye shuts down 50% of that input. If at all possible, shoot with both eyes open.

INDEX

NOTES

NOTES